Fish, Bugs & Birds

For the kids close by: Andrew and Allie,
who inspired us from the start, Mark, Kelsey,
Henning and Anna, for your love, encouragement
and fine outlook on life! With love.
—M.C. & C.C.

I dedicate this book to God
and to my Mom and Dad.
Your encouragement made this happen.
—T.K.

Book 4

GOD's
Creation
SERIES

Fish, Bugs & Birds

Written & Illustrated by

Michael & Caroline Carroll

Cartoons by Travis King

zonderkidz

zonderkidz
The children's group
of Zondervan

www.zonderkidz.com

Book 4: Fish, Bugs & Birds
Text and illustration copyright © 2005 by Michael and Caroline Carroll
Cartoons copyright © 2005 Travis King
Photo on page 8: Rick and Randy Lamutt, Deap Sea Galleries
Photos on page 12 and 28, top: Bill Gerrish
Photos on page 24 and 30 copyright © Dennis Kunkel, PhD

Requests for information should be addressed to:
Zonderkidz, Grand Rapids, Michigan 49530

Library of Congress Cataloging-in-Publication Data

Carroll, Michael W., 1955-
  Fish, bugs & birds / written and illustrated by Michael and Caroline Carroll ; Gnurtley
cartoons by Travis King.– 1st ed.
      p. cm. – (God's creation series ; bk. 4)
  ISBN 0-310-70581-9 (softcover)
  1. Creation–Juvenile literature. 2. Animals–Juvenile literature. [1. Creation. 2. Animals–
Religious aspects–Christianity.] I. Title: Fish, bugs, and birds. II. Carroll, Caroline, 1956- III.
King, Travis ill. IV. Title.
  BS651.C3345 2005
  231.7'65–dc22
                                                                    2003026701

Editor: Barbara Scott
Art direction & design: Laura Maitner-Mason
Production artist: Sarah Jongsma
Cover design: Chris Tobias
Scientific review: Dr. Corrine Carlson
Theological review: Dr. Stanley R. Allaby

Printed in China
05 06 07 08 09/CTC/5 4 3 2 1

A Special Word About

God's Creation Series

God created the heavens and the earth and lots of
other cool stuff too! This series is divided in a way
that is like the creation week described in Genesis,
but we put a few things in different places so we
can understand them better. In Book One we talk
about the beginning of the universe along with the
stars and planets, while the Bible talks about the sun,
moon, and stars on the fourth day. Don't worry—we
noticed! God's Creation Series is about the wonders
of God's creation, and not so much about when each
event took place. So hold on for the ride of your life—
through time and space—to enjoy the great things

God said, "Let there be lights in the expanse of the sky..." And it was so... And there was evening, and there was morning—the fourth day. And God said, "Let the water teem with living creatures, and let birds fly above the earth across the expanse of the sky" ...And there was evening, and there was morning—the fifth day.

—Genesis 1:14-23

The instant God began to create, the universe became an exciting place, exploding with movement, sound, and color. As God put the heavens together, the stars, planets, sun, and moon wheeled across the skies. He separated waters below from waters above, and the skies cleared so that the beings of Earth could see the sun and moon and stars. Now God's creatures below could mark the days, the seasons, and the years.

God made the land rise from the sea and he put plants on the dry ground. The time had come to fill the world with life. On the fifth day, he said, "Let the waters be filled with living things." And as the living things darted and swam through the oceans, clouds of new creatures drifted through the air, some with butterfly wings and googly eyes and some with plumes of feathers and colorful beaks. They splashed and swam, darted and glided, whirred, chirped, and sang through the oceans and skies of God's world.

NOW HEAR THIS! FISH USE THEIR LATERAL LINE TO HELP THEM HEAR SOUND UNDERWATER!

Wild and Wet: God's Own Sea Worlds

There are more fish than all the other animals with backbones in the entire world! Fish live in every kind of water: in the cold seas in the Arctic and Antarctic regions, in the warm waters of the tropics, in salty seawater, and in freshwater streams and lakes.

A drink of fresh air: Fish have a special way to get air out of water. They breathe through gills (slits on the sides of their heads). Water comes in through their mouths, washes through the gills, and then flows out again. Tiny blood vessels in the gills take the oxygen out of the water. Don't try this in the tub,

kids. You don't have gills!

If you look closely at a fish, you will see eyes, a mouth, a "nose," but no ears. Fish have their ears inside their heads. They also have another kind of hearing to help them get around in the 3D environment underwater. Along the sides of their bodies, lie a long line of special scales. This *lateral line* lets them "feel" sound in the water. When a predator is sneaking up from behind, the fish can tell by the vibrations in the water. It's a "sixth sense"! These scales also help them swim close together in schools without running into one other.

Fish in the Bible

God gives us responsibility to take care of creatures living in the sea, lakes, and rivers. The Bible tells us that "...all the fish of the sea; they are given into your hands." (Genesis 9:2). In the same passage, fish are given to people to eat: *"Everything that lives and moves will be food for you"* (Genesis 9:3).

1. Fish were important to Jesus. After his resurrection, Jesus ate fish in front of his disciples (Luke 24:42–43) and fed the disciples a fish breakfast (John 21:9–13)!

2. The Bible talks about catching fish with nets (Ecclesiastes 9:12), hooks (Isaiah 19:8), and spears (Job 41:7).

We see many miracles connected with fish. Here are just a few that you can look up:

1. Jonah 1:17 (Jonah and the big fish)

2. Luke 9:10–17 (loaves and fishes)

3. Matthew 17:27 (coin in the fish's mouth)

4. John 21:6 (the big catch of fish)

The life goals of a fish are simple

1. Find food

2. Reproduce

3. Avoid being eaten by a bigger fish!

Number three is a biggie, and many ocean creatures have weird ways of defending themselves.

There are three kinds of fish

1. *Cartilaginous fish* have no bones. Instead, their "skeletons" are made of cartilage—the same hard stuff that forms your nose and ears. Their skin is leathery. Sharks and rays are cartilaginous fish— no bones about it!

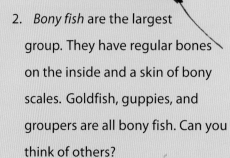

2. *Bony fish* are the largest group. They have regular bones on the inside and a skin of bony scales. Goldfish, guppies, and groupers are all bony fish. Can you think of others?

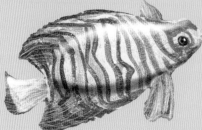

3. The smallest group of fish is the *lungfish*. These strange beasties are able to come up on land and breathe air for short periods.

Aquatic arsenal

1. The blowfish (or puffer) is thin and long until it is frightened. Then it sucks in water and inflates its hollow body like a balloon, blowing itself up to three times its normal size!

2. The butterfly fish has spots on its tail that look like eyes. Since fish usually attack each other head first, this confuses its enemy, which often swims away.

3. The angelfish looks like a colorful flat Frisbee. When this oceanic Houdini is startled, it can turn away so that its thin body nearly disappears. It's so skinny that it can hide in cracks of rock or coral.

4. Some fish can change color to blend in with their surroundings. Seahorses can turn bright red, to match a sponge that they are clinging to, or become the same mottled brown as branches and coral around them.

5. Stingrays have poison-barbed tails that they slash back and forth when something scares them.

6. And then there's our old eight-legged friend, the octopus. This boneless creature is very intelligent, and when startled, it can release a cloud of ink. It swims away, leaving its attacker in a black fog.

Leviathan and creatures of the deep

The Bible speaks of Leviathan in the following passages:

1. Job 41:1–34
2. Isaiah 27:1
3. Psalm 74:14
4. Psalm 104:26

Some people who study the Bible believe that Job 41 is talking about a whale because it speaks of great strength. But other scholars point out that whales are seldom found in the Mediterranean where the Bible was written. Some believe the words apply best to the crocodile, which was abundant in Bible lands and well known to people of Bible times. Still others say Leviathan is a creature that is unknown today, although it is important to remember that the Bible was written as much for us today as for those in the Old and New Testament times.

Leviathan is not the only creature of the deep. There are many mysteries still waiting to be discovered in the deepest seas. Far below the surface of the ocean, there is eternal night. In this constant darkness, some fish make their own light. They have glowing spots on their fins or even little lights that

invite other fish to dinner—to *be* dinner! The anglerfish has a little light that dangles just ahead of wide toothy jaws, which clamp down on anything attracted to his light. The fangtooth is a barbed buddy that chomps on other fish in the total darkness around him.

In Jules Verne's science fiction classic Twenty Thousand Leagues Under the Sea, *giant squids attacks a ship.*

Another strange beast of the deep is the giant squid. Legends have been told for centuries about a sea monster with tentacles that dragged ships to their death, but only recently was evidence found. Whales have been spotted with big sucker marks on their skin, and fishermen pulled up a dead squid that was as long as five cars! A "colossal squid" has also been discovered near Antarctica with eyes as big as dinner plates and hooks on its tentacles! But no one knows how big these bizarre beasties grow, and no one has ever seen one alive.

Question & Answer

QUESTION: What do you call a fish with no eye?

ANSWER: FSH

QUESTION: What's the difference between a fish and a piano?

ANSWER: You can tune a piano but you can't tuna fish.

QUESTION: What is a fish's favorite TV show?

ANSWER: Whale of Fortune

QUESTION: Who held the baby octopus for ransom?

ANSWER: Squid-nappers!

So how do all these deep-sea creatures get food? Close to the sea bottom is a layer of tiny shrimp and other food called zooplankton. The zooplankton forms a layer of yummy stuff called the benthic boundary layer. But below the benthic layer, two miles down, much of the deep-sea floor is like an empty desert. In this seemingly dead place, God has more surprises for us. They're called hydrothermal vents.

Hydrothermal vents are like an Old Faithful geyser at the bottom of the sea. At the edges of those plates that we talked about in *Rocks & Plants* (Book 3), lines of volcanic vents bubble away in the dark. The hottest are called "black smokers," but there are other kinds of vents. The vents grow into tall chimneys that look like melted castles. It's God's deep-sea sculpture garden!

The vents spew minerals into the water. Entire neighborhoods of weird animals live off the minerals that come from the vents. Tube worms wave in the hot water, sifting the minerals from the volcanic stream. Blind crabs scamper about.

The final goal of a fish is to reproduce just as God commanded. Most fish lay eggs. Some fish hold the eggs in their mouths to protect them and even let newly hatched babies stay in their mouths. Seahorses have a new twist on giving birth. The mother lays her eggs in the father's pouch, and the father keeps them inside like a kangaroo until they hatch. Out pop hundreds of live babies!

From sea to sky

Flying fish launch themselves from the water to escape from attackers. Some flying fish can glide farther than the length of a football field! But God did not design these creatures to actually fly. They glide on large fins. To really fly, God created the birds and insects.

13

Fun Facts

In laboratory experiments, Octopuses were given a jar that contained a crab. They figured out how to open the jar. Octopuses are as intelligent as dogs. They can solve puzzles and mazes, and are clever enough to escape their own aquarium to climb into another one when nobody's looking!

"Current" critters

Some eels and catfish put out jolts of electricity to stun an enemy.

The world's hottest animal is the Pompeii worm, which lives in water as hot as 176 degrees Fahrenheit!

Birds: God's Beautiful Creatures of the Sky

God filled the waters with fish and the skies with birds. He really must have loved making birds, since he filled the skies with more than eight thousand kinds of them. Birds are among God's most amazing creatures. He designed each kind of bird with its own special size, shape, color, behavior, call, kind of nest, shape, and color of egg. Wow!

Birds are:

- animals but not mammals
- warm-blooded
- egg-layers
- the only creatures with feathers

Birds help people by:

- eating lots of insects
- eating seeds from weeds
- eating dead animals
- providing food for people

God created birds to fly. How did he do that? Let's look at the miracle of bird design. God designed bird's bones to be light but strong. Inside, the bones are hollow, with struts of thin bone to make them stronger. Engineers copied this strut design to make airplane wings. God covered birds with feathers to protect them from the heat and cold. He also made the feathers light and strong so that birds can fly. As birds flap their wings, the wing feathers close on the down stroke and open on the up stroke. God gave the birds strong flight muscles so they can beat their wings hard enough to get airborne.

Bird brains

Some birds are very smart. The smartest birds are in the parrot family and the crow family. Betty, a New Caledonian crow being studied at Oxford University, figured out how to take a straight wire and bend it into a hook to get food out of a container. This means she is able to use a material she has never seen in the wild to make a tool. Not even chimpanzees can do that!

Romance

In the bird world, the male gets to be the glamour guy. In most bird species, the male, not the female, has the colorful, fancy feathers. He uses these bright feathers to attract a mate. Have you ever seen a male peacock fan out his beautiful tail feathers? He's not doing it for you—he's showing off for the nearest girl!

Many males also sing to attract a mate. Sometimes a male will bring twigs to a female to show her he wants to build a nest with her.

Bringing Up Baby

All birds lay eggs, but each type of bird builds a nest that is uniquely suited to hold its eggs. Some birds build their nests in trees and bushes, while others make nests on the ground. The tailorbird stitches two leaves together to make its nest. The ringed plover makes a dip in the ground, then lines it with stones and shells. Some birds build their nests in handy human items—an old boot, teapot, porch light, or chimney.

Some birds don't make nests at all. In the Antarctic winter, the female emperor penguin lays one egg and then takes off for the sea. There are no materials to make a nest, so the male emperor penguin patiently holds the egg on his feet. This keeps it warm and off the snow. In the spring, the little chick hatches and stands on its father's feet, nestling up against his body to keep warm. Then the female returns from the sea to feed her new baby and give Dad a break!

Usually both parents care for their chick, bringing them food and keeping them warm at night. Feeding the hungry chick is a full-time job. Baby birds often need to eat their body weight in worms, grubs, and insects every day. Many birds care for their babies for months after they hatch. The black-necked swan even carries her babies on her back for safety.

Birds have no teeth. They swallow their food whole. They have gizzards inside their bodies filled with gravel or sand they have swallowed. This gravel acts as "teeth" and grinds up the food.

CARRION MUST FIT UNDER THE SEAT IN FRONT OF YOU.

Bird of Prey: The Bald Eagle

A bird of prey is a bird that hunts other live creatures for food. The bald eagle is one of the most magnificent birds of prey. Bald eagles are not really bald, but have white feathers on their head. The eagle is a wonderful hunter, and can dive at up to one hundred miles per hour to swoop down on his prey. He hunts fish, other birds, and small animals like mice and rabbits. There are even sightings of bald eagles carrying off small dogs. He also eats carrion—dead animals.

Storks know when to fly south. So do doves, swifts and thrushes.

Jeremiah 8:7 (NIrV)

The bald eagle lives near water—coastline, rivers, lakes, and wet prairies—and can be found from Canada to Baja California, in Mexico. The bald eagle can actually swim, using its wings in a butterfly stroke.

Bird Facts

Big birds: The biggest land bird is the ostrich, which lives in Africa and Asia. The ostrich can be up to 9 feet tall and weigh up to 345 pounds. It can't fly, but can run thirty-seven miles per hour—that's as fast as a horse can gallop. An ostrich egg is about 8 inches long and weighs around 3 pounds. That's eighteen chicken eggs!

Tiny birds: The tiniest bird is the bee hummingbird, which lives in Cuba. This tiny creature is two and a half inches long and weighs one-sixteenth of an ounce—less than a dime. Its egg is less than a quarter of an inch long, about the size of an eraser on the end of a pencil.

Hovering birds: Hummingbirds are like tiny, feathered helicopters. They are the only birds that can hover and fly backward, forward, and sideways. They get their name from the humming sound their wings make. The male ruby-throated hummingbird, which lives in North America, beats his wings seventy times per *second*!

Dangerous birds: The cassowary, native to New Guinea and northeastern Australia, is the most dangerous. This bird cannot fly, but it is six-feet tall, with strong legs and sharp claws on its feet. It can leap into the air and kick an attacker to death.

The birds of the air build nests by the waters.
Psalm 104:12 (NIrV)

Commuting birds: The arctic tern migrates back and forth from the Antarctic to the Arctic, a distance of 22,000 miles—the longest of any bird.

Bully birds: The cuckoo bird doesn't make a nest. It just lays its eggs in another bird's nest. When the cuckoo bird hatches, it pushes the other eggs and chicks out of the nest and gobbles up the food brought by the parents.

Grounded birds: There are some birds that cannot fly, like the ostrich, the cassowary, the penguin, and the kiwi.

Cuckoo chick in reed warbler's nest

Talking birds: Some birds, such as the mynah, parakeet, and parrot, are good at imitating sounds and can be taught to repeat words.

WHAT'S SMARTER THAN A TALKING PARROT?
A SPELLING BEE!

Question & Answer

QUESTION: Why do seagulls live near the sea?

ANSWER: Because if they lived near the bay they would be bagels.

QUESTION: What kind of bird does construction work?

ANSWER: The crane.

QUESTION: What do you get when you cross a cat with a parrot:

ANSWER: A carrot!

QUESTION: Why does a flamingo stand on one leg?

ANSWER: Because if he lifted that leg off the ground he would fall!

QUESTION: What do you call a sick bird?

ANSWER: Illegal

QUESTION: Why do birds fly south for the winter?

ANSWER: It's too far to walk!

Not So Fun Fact

Extinction: Close to 600 species of birds have become extinct in the last forty years. This happens because of hunting, loss of habitat, and pollution. There are only about 200 whooping cranes left in the world.

I DARE YOU TO SAY THIS THREE TIMES FAST: BLACK BUGS BLEED BLUE BLOOD, BUT BLUE BUGS BLEED BLACK BLOOD!

"BLACK BUGS BLEED BLUE BLOOD, BUT BLUE BUGS BLEED BLACK BLOOD!"

"BLACK BUGS BLEED BLUE BLOOD, BUT BLUE BUGS BLEED BLACK BLOOD!"

"BLACK BUGS BLEED BLUE BLOOD, BUT BLUE BUGS BLEED BLACK BLOOD!"

"BLACK BUGS BLEED BLUE BLOOD, BUT BLUE BUGS BLEED BLACK BLOOD!"

"BLACK BUGS BLEED BLUE BLOOD, BUT BLUE BUGS BLEED BLACK BLOOD!"

Insects

Birds are an awesome addition to God's zoo, but there are other things on the wing. They are the insects!

Go outside. Look up in the air. Look out at the bushes and trees. Look down at the soil. You're surrounded! Insects are everywhere. More than one million different species of insects crawl, buzz, squirm, and flit across every continent on earth. You can find them under rocks, in trees, on dogs and cats and bats, on the surface of pools, and even in searing deserts and frozen glaciers. It's enough to make a person—well—buggy!

Why not get out the flyswatter and be done with all of them? Well, because bugs are a very important part of God's creation. They are the last link of the food chain, food for birds, fish, and many other animals. Insects spread pollen from many fruit trees and flowering plants, carrying it from one place to another. Pollen helps plants make seeds so that new plants and trees can grow. Without

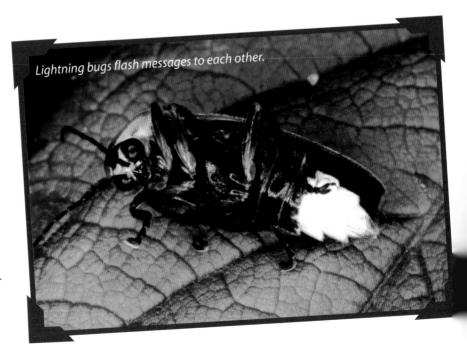
Lightning bugs flash messages to each other.

Scarab beetles come in many beautiful colors.

insects, there would be no fruit or flowers. Insects also make food. Bees make honey for your biscuits.

Many insects bring beauty to our world. Brightly colored butterflies flit through the air, tasting things with their feet and smelling the air with their antennae. Iridescent beetles shine in rainbow colors in the sunlight, and ladybugs add bright orange and black to the green leaves they hang out on. At night, lightning bugs decorate trees like Christmas lights. Insects even bring beauty to the sounds we hear. The chirp of crickets and the song of the cicada bring God's glory to the night.

If you put all of the animal species on earth together, one out of every four would be a beetle. But there's more where that buggy factoid came from. If you could weigh all the world's living things together, ants would make up one tenth of that weight!

Bug Bods

Amazing insects have bodies very different from ours. Insects have no bones. Instead, their skeleton is on the outside in the form of a hard shell (called an exoskeleton). A bug body has three parts: a head, a thorax (the middle part), and an abdomen.

Insect heads

These have all sorts of alien-looking features.

- Insect mouths: If you were an insect, your mouth would be an up-and-down slit from your forehead to your chin, instead of a slit from side to side.
- Insect eyes: Bugs have two kinds of eyes. They have very small eyes called simple eyes, which see in shades of light and dark. Next to their simple eyes, insects have huge compound eyes. Compound eyes are like domes with hundreds of little lenses. Worker ants have as few as 100 of these lenses, but some insects have 28,000. Each lens makes its own little picture. If you were a bug at the ice cream parlor, you could see 28,000 hot fudge sundaes at one time!
- Insect noses: You won't find a nose on a bug. Insects have "smellers" in different places than we do. Flies have "noses" on their feet!

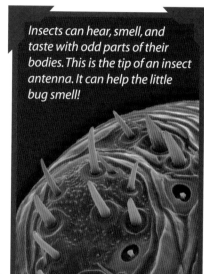

Insects can hear, smell, and taste with odd parts of their bodies. This is the tip of an insect antenna. It can help the little bug smell!

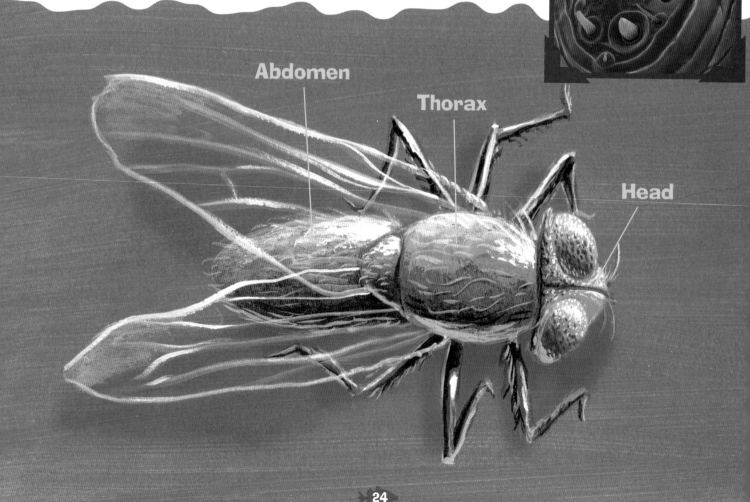

Abdomen

Thorax

Head

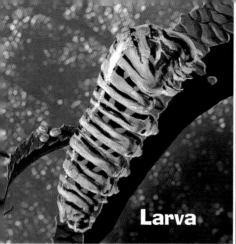

Larva

Chrysalis

Butterfly

Insect heads also have antennae sticking out of the top, which are used for feeling and smelling.

- Insect ears: Listen to this: House crickets listen to sounds with their front legs!

The thorax

This is the chest area of the bug. Sometimes the thorax is called the "engine room" of an insect, because it has all the things that move a bug around. All insects have six legs, which sprout from the thorax. The thorax is also the part of the body from which the wings grow.

The abdomen

This is the section below the thorax. It holds most of an insect's guts. Right now, you are breathing with your lungs—bags of air inside your chest. Lungs are big in the animal world. Cats, dogs, frogs, ducks, hedgehogs, and everything else that breathes air does it with lungs. Everything, that is, except insects.

Insects have holes in the sides of their bodies called spiracles that bring air inside through smaller and smaller pipes. Some insects even breathe through their skin. But that's just the beginning of bug-gut bizarreness.

Insects have no veins or arteries to carry their blood through their bodies. Instead, a simple heart along the back pumps greenish blood, which sloshes around inside the body. Yep, insects have weird bodies, but those bodies are designed to work beautifully in the world of bugs.

Metamorphosis

A human baby looks like a tiny adult, with little arms and legs and everything else. But a baby butterfly doesn't look like a tiny butterfly. It has no wings and lots of suction-cup feet. A baby butterfly is a caterpillar!

Many insect babies look quite different from their parents. As they grow, they go through several stages that look nothing like their parents. These steps together are called metamorphosis.

Question & Answer

QUESTION: What do you get when you cross a rabbit with an insect?

ANSWER: Bugs Bunny

QUESTION: What has four wheels and flies?

ANSWER: A garbage truck.

QUESTION: What is the best kind of computer bug?

ANSWER: Spiders. They make the best web sites.

HA HA HA HA HA

The first stage, fresh out of the egg, is called the larva. A butterfly larva is a caterpillar. A caterpillar eats and grows—that's its job in life. Its skin is tough and leathery, and it doesn't grow. Instead, the caterpillar's skin splits and falls off several times as the caterpillar gets bigger. After it gets big enough, the caterpillar spins a hard shell around itself. This shell is called a chrysalis (moths spin the same kind of thing, and it's called a cocoon). The caterpillar inside is now in the pupa stage. The pupa sleeps within this cocoon for weeks or even months. Finally, the chrysalis splits and out climbs a beautiful butterfly!

Other insects go through metamorphosis too. The larva of a dragonfly lives under water and breathes through gills, like a fish. For two years, it hunts other insects and even small fish. It sheds its skin fifteen times and then climbs out onto a leaf, where it crawls out of its last skin as a dragonfly.

Bible illustration

Many artists who paint religious pictures use the butterfly as a symbol for Jesus. Like the caterpillar, Jesus went into a sort of cocoon when he died. He was inside the tomb for three days but then came out again— reborn. The butterfly seems to be reborn, as Jesus was, and just as we can be when the Spirit of God gives us new life. Through Jesus, we can spread our wings and fly through life more freely than we could before we met God.

Bees in Bible times

Bees were important to people in Bible times, just as they are to us today. Honey from beehives was used to sweeten food. To the Israelites, honey was a very good thing! The Promised Land was described as *"a land flowing with milk and honey"* (Exodus 3:8), and the psalmist described the Word of God as *"sweeter than honey that is taken from the honeycomb"* (Psalm 19:10, 119:103, NIrV). Bees have been kept for their honey since ancient times.

A bee will sometimes sting an intruder. Only female bees have stingers. Why doesn't the poison in a bee stinger make a bee sick? It's because the poison is made by mixing chemicals together. The chemicals mix only as the bee jabs its stinger into its victim. It really isn't poison until it leaves the bee's body.

Bees live in "cities" called hives. There are places to eat and sleep, places to store food, and even a sort of control center where the queen bee lives, spending her life laying eggs. Worker bees guard the hive and feed the newly hatched beebies. There may be 60,000 worker bees in one hive! Worker bees are always females. They are the bees that leave the nest to get nectar from flowers. Workers bring it back to the hive to make bee-food (honey). Worker bees can do a special dance to tell the other bees where they have discovered nectar.

The male bees stay at the hive. They mate with the queen so she can lay eggs. The queen bee is the only bee that can lay eggs. She is twice as large as the other bees, because when she was a baby, she was fed a special food called royal jelly made by the worker bees. She is pampered and fed all day by the other bees. The worker bees build thousands of six-sided cubicles made of wax. The queen lays an egg in each. Finally, when the hive becomes crowded, the queen leads some of the other bees to build a new hive.

Grasshoppers

If you live near a grassy place, you've probably seen grasshoppers. They have strong jaws for eating tough veggies. They have four legs for walking and two strong hind legs for jumping. Most grasshoppers have a pair of wings for flying and another pair that act as a protective shield when they are resting or hopping. Grasshoppers are usually the same color as the

IN A SMALL SWARM OF 50 MILLION, LOCUSTS CAN EAT ENOUGH FOOD TO FEED 500 PEOPLE FOR AN ENTIRE YEAR.

plants they like to hang out in, but often they have brightly colored wings to scare away enemies when they fly.

Locusts

These are like big grasshoppers. One of the ten plagues of Egypt was the plague of locusts (Exodus 10:1–19). Deuteronomy 28:38 (NIrV) tells us, *"You will plant many seeds in your field. But you will gather very little food. Locusts will eat it up."* It's no wonder that people fear these greedy super-grasshoppers. They strip entire crops to dust as they flock through the air. In Africa, swarms of desert locusts are made up of 28 billion (not thousand, not million, but *billion*) bad bugs. Together, they weigh 70,000 tons or about as much as 55,000 cars!

Insects like this housefly have compound eyes made of many tiny lenses.

Mosquitoes

Mosquitoes suck out blood and leave a bite!

As you probably know, mosquitoes are not very popular at picnics, because they bite people. Their noses are like hypodermic needles, and they slip them into your skin without you knowing. After they suck out a little blood, they leave. But by then, they have given you something to remember them by—an itchy bite! A female mosquito may bite as many as eighteen people in one hour. Sometimes their bites can give people diseases like malaria and West Nile virus.

Mosquitoes lay their eggs in water. When the larvae hatch, they live in the water for three weeks. Then they turn into adult mosquitoes and fly away to picnics.

Flies

These icky insects can fly twenty-five miles per hour! Flies have compound eyes with 4,000 six-sided lenses. They can see almost all the way around themselves but not far into the distance. Instead, they have hairs all over that sense vibration, so the moving air of a flyswatter warns them that they are about to have a smashing day. Flies have sticky pads on the bottoms of their feet so they can walk on glass windows or even

IF YOU WANT TO SWAT A FLY YOU SHOULD ATTACK IT FROM BEHIND. FLIES CAN'T SEE BEHIND THEMSELVES.

on your ceiling. A single housefly may carry a million bacteria on its body, so it can cause sickness.

A fly is able to take off in one-thousandth of a second and accelerate at a speed that is thirty times faster than the speed experienced by a space-shuttle astronaut during launch.

Other bug-like creatures

God created a whole lot of other things to crawl around on the ground. Eight-legged spiders that spin magnificent webs, glow-in-the-dark scorpions with stinging tails, and leggy centipedes that slither through your garden—these are just a few of the numerous creatures God has put into the world. And what about dirt, you ask? Earthworms make rich soil for the plants to grow in.

Spider

Earthworm

Scorpion

Centipede

Amaze your friends with these fun bug facts:

- A cockroach can live for nine days without its head.
- Ants work together to build underground colonies. Ants can pull objects eleven times their own weight. The black ant squirts acid on its enemies!

- Dragonflies can fly at speeds up to sixty-five miles per hour, with their wings beating thirty times every second.
- The biggest bug: The rare South American longhorn beetle is over 6 ½ inches long. That's as long as a pencil!
- The smallest bug: The fairy fly is smaller than the period at the end of this sentence.
- The stick insect is more than fourteen inches long. That's the size of a loaf of bread.
- The biggest wings: Some butterflies have wings a foot across, as big as a dinner plate. You think that's big? Fossils of giant dragonflies have wings nearly a meter across—about the size of a grown up's arm!
- The most poisonous bug: The South African velvet ant, also called the mutillid wasp.
- Out-of-the-way bugs: Brine flies live in weird places, such as pools of oil, hot springs in Iceland, and the salty water of Mono Lake.
- Million-mite march: A scientist once found that in one acre of pasture in Britain, there were 400 million insects and 666 million mites.

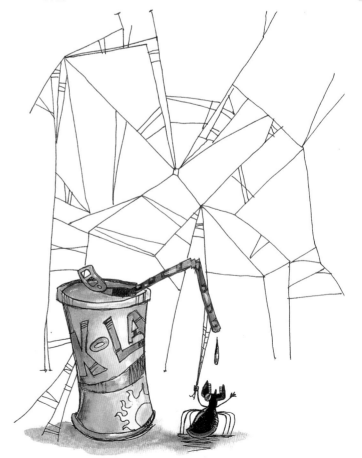

IF YOU WERE A FLEA, YOU COULD JUMP 150 TIMES AS FAR AS YOUR HEIGHT!

• Caffeinated critters: In the 1960s, researchers fed spiders different substances in an experiment. Caffeine-fed spiders spun uneven webs. Spiders that were given sedatives fell asleep before they could finish their webs!

• Octopus of the insect world: The bombardier beetle defends itself by firing a boiling hot spray at its enemy. The spray is created by mixing together two chemicals. As these chemicals meet, they instantly turn to a hot gas, which the beetle squirts out to irritate the eyes of its enemy. The spray also acts like a smoke screen so the beetle can make a clean getaway.

Bombardier beetles have a built-in weapon.

Insects are among God's most bizarre and cool creatures! But they are just part of the vast design of God's living world, the earth. As the fifth day dawned, the world saw the sun, moon, and stars shining down from the heavens, but there were no creatures to feel the warm sunlight, peer out in the moonlight, or sing under the stars. God brought forth living things that crawl, scamper, swim, and fly. Like the rest of his creation, these creatures are a signpost showing the way to a great and loving creator. But the creative God of the universe wasn't finished yet. He had plans for even more creatures. On the sixth day, God brought forth the animals of the land—monkeys, mongooses, turkeys, turtles, crocodiles, camels, and eventually—you and me!

Index

Africa 18, 29
Antarctica 8, 11, 16, 19
Arctic 8, 19
Australia 18
Asia 18
Baja California, Mexico 18
benthic boundary layer........... 12
Bible......................... 5, 9, 11, 28
birds
  food.................................... 15
  types
    arctic tern...................... 19
    bald eagle.................. 16–18
    bee............................... 28
    bee hummingbird 18
    black-necked swan 16
    cassowary 18–19
    chicken........................... 18
    crane 20
    cuckoo 19
    dove 17
    emperor penguin 16, 19
    flamingo........................ 20
    hummingbird 18
    kiwi............................... 19
    mynah 19
    New Caledonian crow 15
    ostrich...................... 18–19
    parakeet 19
    parrot........................ 19–20
    peacock 16
    reed warbler.................... 19
    ringed plover................... 16
    ruby-throated
      hummingbird 18
    seagull........................... 20
    stork 17
    swift.............................. 17
    tailorbird....................... 16
    thrush 17
    whooping cranes 20
black smokers 12
  see also hydrothermal vents
Britain................................... 32
Canada................................... 18
cocoon 26
compound eyes......................... 24
crab 12, 13
Creation...................... 5, 22, 34
crocodile 11
Cuba 18

Deuteronomy 29
Earth 7
Ecclesiastes............................... 9
Egypt...................................... 29
Exodus 28–29
exoskeleton 23
fish
  kinds
    cartilaginous 9
    bony................................. 9
    lungfish 9
  types
    angelfish 10
    anglerfish 11
    blowfish 10
    butterfly 10
    fangtooth 11
    flying.............................. 13
    goldfish 9
    groupers........................... 9
    guppies............................. 9
Frisbee.................................... 10
Genesis................................. 5, 9
God 5, 7, 8, 9, 12, 13,
         15, 22, 23, 26, 28, 34
Houdini.................................. 10
hydrothermal vents 12
  see also black smokers
Iceland 32
insects
  body 25
  types
    ant 24, 32
    beetle 23
    bombardier beetle 33
    brine fly 32
    butterfly 25
    caterpillar.................. 25–26
    centipede 31
    cicada............................ 23
    cockroach 32
    cricket 23, 25
    dragonfly 26, 32
    earthworm 31
    fairy fly 32
    grasshopper..................... 29
    housefly 24, 30–31
    ladybug.......................... 23
    lightning bug................... 23
    locust 29
    mosquito......................... 30

mutillid wasp 32
  see also South African
    velvet ant
moth 26
scorpion 31
spider 31, 33
South African velvet ant... 32
  see also mutillid wasp
South American
  longhorn beetle 32
stick 32
Isaiah 9, 11
Israelites 28
Jesus................................... 9, 26
Job 9, 11
John 9
Jonah 9
lateral line 8
Leviathan 11
Luke... 9
Matthew 9
Mediterranean 11
Mono Lake 32
moth 26
New Guinea 18
New Testament 11
North America 18
octopus 10, 13, 33
Old Faithful 12
Old Testament......................... 11
Oxford University 15
Pompeii worm......................... 13
Promised Land 28
Psalm 11, 28
pupa....................................... 26
royal jelly 28
seahorses 10, 13
shrimp.................................... 12
simple eyes 24
squid 11
stingrays 10
tube worms 12
Twenty Thousand Leagues
  Under the Sea 11
Verne, Jules 11
West Nile 30
whale 11
Word 28
zooplankton............................ 12

GOD's Creation SERIES

BOOK 1

Space & Time

zonderkidz

Written & Illustrated by Michael & Caroline Carroll
Cartoons by Travis King

I DARE YOU TO SAY THIS THREE TIMES FAST:
BLACK BUGS BLEED BLUE BLOOD, BUT BLUE BUGS BLEED BLACK BLOOD!

God's Creation Series

Written & Illustrated by Michael and Caroline Carroll

Cartoons by Travis King

Kids will enjoy learning about creation with this set of books—for ages 6 & up

Cartoons, artistic renderings, photographs, fun facts, and more make these informative and entertaining books on creation a rich visual experience— while presenting scientific information.

Space & Time
Book 1
ISBN: 0-310-70578-9

Rocks & Plants
Book 3
ISBN: 0-310-70580-0

Sky & Sea
Book 2
ISBN: 0-310-70579-7

Fish, Bugs & Birds
Book 4
ISBN: 0-310-70581-9